To: Alison

I hope you enjoy the above your Pink Clouds.

- BréAnna ♡

MW00930503

Pink Clouds

An Interactive Journal Designed
for Teen Girls by a Teen Girl

BréAnna A. G. Smith

ISBN: 978-1-71693-593-0 (sc)
ISBN: 978-1-71692-897-0 (hc)
ISBN: 978-1-71693-591-6 (e)

Library of Congress Control Number: 2020902626

National Suicide Prevention Lifeline: 800-273-8255

Please consider gifting or donating a book to support a teen as she rises above her pink clouds. For more information or to order in bulk for special groups, organizations, or schools, please contact us at sonyceinc777@gmail.com

Lulu Publishing Services rev. date: 05/30/2020

To my parents, who have supported me throughout this 4 year writing journey.

Contents

Foreword

Pink clouds are beautiful to behold. However, various forms of air pollution in the environment combine to create a pink cloud. Pink clouds could be considered a combination of unwanted residue, toxins, and combustion. The title *Pink Clouds* was derived from an idea that paralleled adolescent experiences associated with girls in middle school and high school. These inevitable adolescent real-life experiences can feel and appear to be insurmountable. However, they can be conquered with appropriate guidance and tools from counselors and professional therapists.

—Dr. Sheri S. Brownlee

Girls have similar social, emotional, and developmental experiences. Some daily occurrences inevitably become life changing. These encounters breed different individual outcomes.

BréAnna, the author of this reflective story and journal, aims to provide a snapshot of actions, responsive approaches, reactions from her perspectives, and accountings of actual events. Her intentions are to share her personal experiences and invite you to reflect and journal about your experiences as a way of promoting higher levels of social emotional awareness. Her responses are a direct result of her battle with "pink clouds."

Pink clouds, a term that we created, refers to personal obstacles; encounters with societal influences; and situations, internal battles, and problems experienced during a specific moment in life. BréAnna's specific set of tools that enable her to conquer her pink clouds were developed, acquired, learned, and enhanced by prayer, parental interactions, family support, and a circle of mentors and positive role models, as well as professional guidance and therapy provided by Makini Austin, LPC.

Frederick O. and Dr. Sheri S. Brownlee

Preface

I began writing this journal in 2016. In the beginning, it was simply a punishment task that I was trying to finish. But throughout these past years, my mindset has drastically changed. The stories that I share are real experiences that I hope will motivate countless teenage girls. I was inspired to write this book to encourage and to provide opportunities for other girls to journal, input their personal pink clouds, and realize that we are more similar than we are different.

Pink Clouds is a testimonial journal about the everyday challenges that I face as a teenage girl. Pink Clouds is a tool that has not only helped me, but it also describes my own personal journey and successes. And it has the power and potential to help anyone who submerges themselves in the journaling process throughout this book.

Writing this book had been like a roller coaster ride. There have been ups and down but through all of the crying and jumping for joy, I was able to learn the real purpose of writing this book. The purpose is to help others that are going through the daily struggles of adolescence. I can say from my multiple encounters with pink clouds that it is difficult going through all of this stress as our bodies are changing and developing. It was definitely difficult writing this book, mentally and emotionally. Finishing this journal has been a personally impactful accomplishment. My writing continues as I am completing Pink Clouds 2, still making mistakes and facing new pink clouds.

Overall, it has been a hard and difficult road. In the end, I'm happy that I wrote this book and had the chance to overcome my own obstacles. In the mist of me helping myself, I am glad that I will be able to provide helpful insight to others.

Introduction

Me, Myself, and I

I'm sure you're wondering what pink clouds are. Pink clouds seem beautiful and fun from a distance, but once you experience them, they can be challenging to overcome since we are still developing as teenagers. In this book they symbolize some of the problems girls may face growing up, including bullying, peer pressure, the dark side of social media, self-doubt, life challenges, and sometimes even understanding yourself.

I hope that reading, journaling, and embracing the messages in this book will give you the power to overcome the pink clouds in your life. Sometimes I find myself in unfamiliar territory that I don't know how to handle. My inspiration for writing this book came from one pink-cloud experience that I will share at the beginning of chapter 1.

I always feel like I don't fit in because of remarks I've heard from other girls growing up. Other girls have said positive and negative things about me, but the negative comments seem to have a lasting effect. I've been teased and humiliated because of my hair, height, smile, personality, and ideas. These are examples of my pink clouds. I've also been complimented and rewarded because of my beauty, determination, and intelligence. It's difficult, but I must learn to ignore the negativity and cherish the positive remarks.

I had to realize that these pink clouds aren't true unless I tell myself they are. I'm sharing my experiences and the lessons I learned from them. I've learned that life is full of mini and giant pink clouds, but it's your choice to decide whether the outcomes define you. It's your choice to rise above the clouds, get lost in them, or run away from them.

Journal about your pink clouds and then talk to someone about them.

I don't talk about my problems.

My Grandma Dollie always told me that sticks and stones may break my bones, but words would never hurt me. Unfortunately, words may not leave a visible mark, but they can scar your heart forever. Whether you let those words affect you is your decision. Sometimes bullies say mean things to try to put you down. They do this to boost their own self-confidence and degrade the confidence of everyone else.

Create a list of your pink clouds. Write about and reflect on an experience where you rose above a pink-cloud situation, such as teasing, bullying, or peer pressure. Remember, God made us all different, flaws and all. We're all amazing just the way we are, no matter what anyone says.

_____

_____

_____

_____

_____

_____

_____

_____

_____

_____

_____

_____

_____

_____

_____

_____

_____

_____

_____

This book was written for everyone, whether or not you realize your problems. I hope and pray this book will help you in one way or another. Life will never be perfect. Even if your life is filled with happiness, you'll still have problems. We all do. To have a happy life, you must deal with the problems head on.

If there were no mistakes, what would be the point of living? If everything always went your way, you'd never learn life lessons. Mistakes, suffering (going without), and conflict help me grow as a person. Mistakes are a natural part of learning and growing up. And I've made my fair share. I remind myself that it's okay to make mistakes. I strive to be honest and live with my imperfections, which isn't easy.

I see suffering as a way of being able to take time to reflect and be content and appreciative. I volunteer at a food bank where we package meals at Open Hand Atlanta. Volunteering has helped me become grateful for what I have. I realize how blessed and fortunate I am. I have a family who provides me with everything I need.

One important life lesson I learned involved conflict. One of my first experiences with conflict was in the fifth grade. When I was nine, my two closest friends were Zoey and Jada. Zoey and I continuously debated over who was Jada's best friend. Being involved in conflicts led me to realize that everyone has a different perspective and perception. When interacting with people in general, there will eventually be conflict.

Be yourself because being fake is masking your true self and will prevent you from being who you really are. In middle school, I felt like I didn't fit in. I realized that for others to accept me, I had to learn to accept myself first with the help of my family and therapist, Makini Austin.

You should want people to accept you for who you are. I want to encourage you to love and accept yourself. We are all different; we contribute to society in different ways. Our uniqueness makes each and every one of us stand out. Our differences make us special. Some people are quiet, some are great at sports, and some know how to make you smile; some people are smart, some are nice, some are good at computers, some are creative, some are good at dance, some are good cooks, and some are determined. This balances out the world. Don't be afraid to show your gifts to the world.

Write some of the reasons you're strong, beautiful, and amazing.

Chapter 1

Trending

- - - - - - - - - - - - - - - - - -

This generation has become technology Zombies

Some social media sites are designed for communication but are used for other purposes by most teens. I should know; I abused it myself. This was one of my many mistakes dealing with social media.

Remember the pink-cloud experience that inspired this testimonial journal that I mentioned in the introduction? Well this is it. One summer, I decided to download a popular texting app. I created a group chat with my friends. One of the girls named Amber added other people to the chat. I took them out, but Amber put them back in again.

We continued that pattern, so she made a whole new chat with me in it. There were some very inappropriate things being said in this chat, but because of my desire to want to fit in, I stayed in the chat.

One day, my mom asked to see my phone for a phone check; I was very nervous. I knew I'd done something wrong. I thought my heart was going to burst out of my chest because I'd lied to her. I gave her my phone anyway. When I texted on the app and she asked what I was doing, I'd say, "Texting my friend," which was only sort of true.

When she looked at the text messages and saw the inappropriate messages, I got yelled at. Not just because of what I did but because I'd lied about it. She took my phone away. When she had my phone, I never asked any questions about it because I was ashamed, and I didn't even want to start the conversation with her.

After a month of not having my phone, she said she was

considering giving it back but that she had to discuss it with my dad first. He decided I shouldn't get my phone back.

Then I went to leadership camp for a month. Campers are not allowed to have their phones, so I wasn't too concerned about not having it.

When I returned from camp, I got my phone back. I did the most logical thing after not having your phone for a whole two months because of text messages—I checked my messages. Just kidding! As soon as I got my phone back, I deleted the app so quickly that I didn't even have time to check my messages.

I realized that fitting in wasn't even worth the trouble. I should be a leader and be different instead, which sometimes means standing alone.

I understand that it's uncomfortable to stand alone, and I'm still developing and learning how to rise above the pink clouds of peer pressure. Ms. Makini and I work together to create strategies that support me as I deal with my pink clouds. The message in this story is that there are going to be things and people in your life that will come and go. Ask yourself, Is it worth the trouble?

Name your favorite type of social media, and name a time when it got you into trouble. Reflect on the lesson you learned and how it changed you as a person.

_____

_____

_____

_____

_____

_____

_____

_____

_____

_____

_____

_____

_____

_____

_____

_____

_____

_____

_____

_____

_____

_____

Going through all that trouble because of a phone may seem like it's worth it but, in the end, it isn't. I understand that our lives revolve around technology and social media, but we must realize that sometimes we just have to put the phone down and interact in real life.

Make a "pail list" of things that you want to do before you leave middle school or high school.

1) _____

2) _____

3) _____

4) _____

5) _____

6) _____

7) _____

"Kik" the phone away, or "Snap" out of the mind-set that you always need a phone.

We must realize that we can't always depend on technology. Because the moment you stop "trending," life will feel incomplete. So leave your phone at home occasionally when you go to school or meet up with a friend in person instead of just seeing his or her face on a screen. Just try it, and maybe you'll start "trending" in real life.

Chapter 2

Mirror, Mirror on the Wall

When you wake up in the morning and look in the mirror, what do you think about? Am I too short? Am I too tall? Is my nose too big? Are my eyes too small? I won't lie; I think of some of these things. But what can I do about them? Absolutely *nothing*. I can't change the fact I'm "too short" or my head is "weirdly shaped." But I can change how I feel about these things.

Am I supposed to sit and cry my eyes out? Or am I going to love myself for who I am and not care what the haters say about me?

Name some things you love about yourself. Why?

_____

_____

_____

_____

_____

_____

_____

_____

_____

_____

_____

_____

_____

_____

_____

_____

_____

_____

_____

_____

_____

_____

Everyone has flaws. My mom always told me that those who bully others are the ones with low self-esteem. There is no need to be concerned about how you look, because God made us all different for a reason. He wanted us to have a chance to see the beauty within ourselves and others.

I'll admit that I'm a short, skinny girl. Sometimes I wish I blended in better, but if I did, then I'd be like everyone else.

Middle school and high school can appear to be cruel places where everyone thinks they must be perfect in order to fit in. I wear a hoodie to school almost every day because it's my style. If people think I'm too basic, that's their opinion. I like wearing them. But there's no such thing as perfect no matter how hard you try.

It is hard to imagine, but your beauty is deep within you. Knowing you're beautiful just strengthens the feeling of ultimate confidence. If you believe in the idea of your own beauty, then you don't need anyone else's approval. If you expect anyone else to believe in you, you must first believe in yourself.

Always look in the mirror and tell yourself that you're the most beautiful of them all. If we all think that, then we don't have to worry about anyone else's opinion.

Chapter 3

Follow the Leader within You

Be the one to Lead the Followers

The RIGHT Way

I love showcasing my leadership style to others. Being a leader isn't about simply bossing everyone around; it's about encouraging others to do great things. Overall, being a leader starts with being able to do the right thing and thinking of yourself as a role model. I'm not saying there's anything wrong with following the right people, but leadership begins with leading yourself. Make your own choices, and don't let others boss you around or lead you to make decisions that have negative consequences.

Leadership is a great quality to possess. Personally, I perceive leadership based on my own experiences with leadership camp, social events, and school-based leadership opportunities. This personal perspective of leadership involves the three Es: enthusiasm, endurance, and emotional stability.

While in a leadership position, it's key to maintain enthusiasm. A positive attitude is essential so your peers can follow your lead and be excited as well. For example, I see teachers as leaders, and if a teacher is apathetic, students will not be excited to learn. At leadership camp, the counselors sometimes become angry or frustrated. Their negativity becomes "contagious," and the campers become angry and frustrated as well. Effective leaders understand that the energy they give off is the energy they're going to receive in return.

As a leader, there will be challenges that you must help your team work through. Endurance is an important skill that is needed to overcome these challenges. It will seem frustrating, but it's the leader's job to help the team through the struggles without letting negative feelings affect the goal. For example, when I went hiking, the counselor was singing songs and telling jokes to prevent people from getting upset and crying. We had been walking for hours in the rain without food. We were all terrified. It's a leader's job to be tolerant and promote a positive attitude within a group.

In order to become a successful leader, you must be able to adequately handle emotions and stress. In other words, you must have emotional stability. I've met my fair share of leaders who think that in order for them to lead, they must yell and scream at everyone. All that does is cause problems because no one likes being yelled at. Yelling evokes emotions such as anger, fear, and frustration. Great leaders will evoke emotions such as happiness, trust, and comfort.

To be a successful leader, you must have enthusiasm, endurance, and emotional stability. Leadership can't be forced but it can be developed. It's a leader's responsibility to not only lead others but to help others lead as well.

Name a time that you felt like a leader. Pick one of the three Es (enthusiasm, endurance, emotional stability) and share how you incorporated it into your leadership experience.

_____

_____

_____

_____

_____

_____

_____

_____

_____

_____

_____

_____

_____

_____

_____

_____

_____

_____

_____

_____

_____

_____

_____

_____

_____

_____

Leadership is about doing the right thing simply because you should. If you cheat and give your friend the answers on a test, what kind of friend are you? I used to be that girl who always felt like I had to follow someone. This led me to feel constricted to following someone else instead of branching out and being myself.

You should always be aware of the example you're setting for your peers. I was a victim of "fake friends" and "falling in with the crowd," but I learned very quickly that I was getting *nowhere* by doing that.

Name five qualities that are similar to those of a leader.

1) _____

2) _____

3) _____

4) _____

5) _____

By understanding your leadership style, it shows how much of a leader you really are. Even if you're not a leader, it's still okay. Everyone can at least be a leader of themselves, even if you started as a follower. If anything, you should follow the leader within yourself. Challenging yourself is trying to be the leader that even the leaders want to follow.

Chapter 4
Block the Haters

- -

It's hard to imagine, but the biggest bully can be the one within yourself. Most bullies go around tormenting people just to ignore their own pain, guilt, and sorrow.

Some bullies are normal people who deal with problems the wrong way, but it didn't matter. I was scared of them.

Whenever someone finds the pain in their heart to bully others, I pray that they'll find the beauty within themselves and not the ugly within others. I know it's often not them talking but their broken heart.

NERD, Ugly, werido

Some people think bullying is funny. *No!* Bullying is nowhere near funny. Ruining someone's life isn't funny. Killing people's dreams is not funny. Making someone feel like he or she should take his or her own life is definitely not funny.

Bullying isn't acceptable, whether it's cyberbullying or mentally or physically bullying. I have been bullied mentally. I've mentally bullied myself as well. I was always told that I was too skinny or too short or too smart and eventually I began to believe them. I was bullied by others. I was teased because of my height, weight, and squeaky voice. As I grew older, I realized the only reason they bully is for the satisfactory of knowing they're not the only ones who are upset.

Reacting to bullies gives them satisfaction, and it makes them continue to bully you and others. Bullies make you feel like you're not important.

Everyone is different in all kinds of ways. Never denigrate yourself because of what someone else said. We just need to come together and accept all our differences.

Be yourself no matter what. I know how it feels to be called different, but I can tell anyone that I'm proud of who I am because God made me the way I am for a reason, and I'm unlike any other no matter what. I've been told what people thought was wrong with my hair, body, face, and voice, but I had to let it in one ear and come out the other. I had to understand if they had to talk about me, they have a lot of problems.

Bullying isn't right, but that doesn't mean people don't do it.

Write about a time you were bullied and how it made you feel.

PINK CLOUDS

Chapter 5

Bottled Up

- -

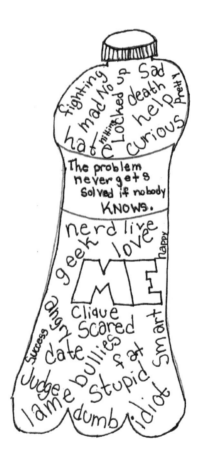

Going through life feeling different from everyone else, I've learned two things. People will talk about you no matter what, and it's never healthy to keep your feelings bottled up. No matter how hard you try, you'll never feel better if you try to keep in your feelings and emotions.

This tends to lead to taking your frustration out on not just others but yourself. Just because you're feeling sad, angry, upset, or confused, you shouldn't take your anger out on others by yelling and screaming at them. Don't take your anger out on yourself by cutting yourself or trying to commit suicide. In the long run, you'll learn that cutting and yelling will never help with the feelings. And suicide is never the answer. There is at least one person in your life at this moment who would never get over your death.

As a child, I never had anger management problems, but I learned the effects of it. I was always teased and sometimes still am about my height as a 5ft 2 11th grader but now I have realized that all they are trying to do is let their anger and frustration out on others. In these types of situations, the best thing to do is get help from an adult or even a therapist. Even though this isn't always the case, you'd be surprised at how many people have this problem.

Anger is an effective way to express your feelings, but anger is not always the only option. I often wonder what life would be like without anger or fear or sadness, but it's impossible to think of a world filled not with hate but with joy.

Let out your anger, but do it the right way. Write in a journal or ask your parents if you could meet with a therapist or your school counselor.

Trust me—it helps. Being afraid to express your feelings can make the situation worse. But staying bottled up isn't just about feeling a certain way but about keeping secrets, which can come back and haunt you with guilt. I always thought you kept secrets to prevent drama, but I now understand that secrets just make the drama even *worse*. Ms. Makini gives me different techniques and tools to help cope with my pink clouds dealing with drama. She tells me there's nothing I can do about bullies and gossipers except be myself and keep my head up.

Name three times when you kept secrets, especially secrets from your parents. Being bottled up isn't the best feeling, so try to avoid it.

1) _____

2) _____

3) _____

Name a time you felt bottled up.

_____

_____

_____

_____

_____

_____

_____

_____

_____

_____

_____

_____

_____

_____

_____

PINK CLOUDS

Chapter 6

Selfie Time

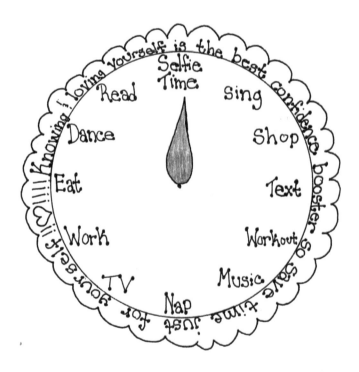

In order to be great, you must believe in yourself first. You must find the awesomeness within. It took me a while to figure out who I was and why I was here. I realized I was a gift from God no matter what anyone else said.

I knew inside my big heart that I was ready to shine. Believing starts with ignoring the bully within you and others.

If you're able to do that, you'll be able to conquer the world. I used to doubt myself until I realized it was getting me nowhere. Believing in yourself will help you achieve many things. I started a habit of waking up, going to the mirror, and complimenting myself.

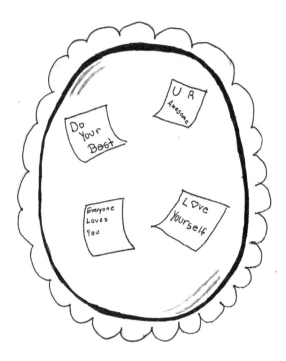

Name five positive things you'll tell yourself in the mirror (one for each week day).

1) _____

2) _____

3) _____

4) _____

5) _____

I often receive compliments, but they can be overpowered by the one hurtful remark made to my face or said behind my back. The worst kind of bullies, including cyberbullies, are the ones who can't say these negative things about you to your face.

I learned the hard way that doing something about that type of bully makes you feel great socially and emotionally. In order to become great, you can't change yourself for other people. You only live once. That's why you should remember and cherish everything about yourself, including the positive and negative things, because those moments are the most significant and special ones in your life. I believe that talking to people face-to-face, not phone to phone, gives people the opportunity to truly connect with others.

Write why you do or don't like social media.

_____

_____

_____

_____

_____

_____

_____

_____

_____

_____

_____

_____

_____

_____

_____

_____

_____

_____

_____

_____

_____

_____

_____

_____

I think social media tears people away from the fact they can develop greatness by themselves and without a phone or computers. It is possible if we as a community choose to believe it's possible. You have to realize that you can have selfie time without technology.

Chapter 7

You Are Beautiful inside and Out

- -

Elegance is when the inside is as beautiful as the outside
—CHANEL

In order to be beautiful, intelligent, special or friendly, you must see it in yourself first. If you don't recognize it and put yourself out there, no one will ever know. Whatever you do, don't try to be something because someone told you to.

I tried to lower my standard for friendship, and it did nothing but degrade my self-confidence. My "friends" ignored me or disrespected me, and I tried to convince myself that it was okay because I wanted the friendship. I realized I deserved a real friendship, with mutual respect and happiness. It was hard to move on, but my support system helped me rise above the heartbreak of this pink cloud.

Describe a time you experienced a "pink cloud heartbreak."

_____

_____

_____

_____

_____

_____

_____

_____

_____

_____

_____

_____

_____

_____

_____

_____

You have the power to be whomever you want because God created you that way, so when someone compliments you, take it to heart. If others call you ugly and you still call them "friends," they really aren't your friends.

I must remind myself that I am beautiful inside and out, even if no one else is going to. There are two types of beauty, inner and outer. Inner beauty starts in your heart. Even if you aren't the prettiest, you can still be beautiful. Outer beauty is just your appearance. That would mean you just *look* pretty; it doesn't necessarily mean you're nice.

Why do you think you're beautiful?

_____

_____

_____

_____

_____

_____

_____

_____

_____

_____

_____

_____

_____

_____

_____

_____

_____

_____

_____

_____

My Grandma Dollie always tells me you can have inner and outer beauty, which is when you look and feel pretty inside and out. Others may not feel the same way about your appearance, but as long as you love yourself, then you're beautiful.

When I say I'm beautiful, I don't feel as if I am being conceited. I feel as if I know how to appreciate myself, and knowing you're beautiful is a great feeling. Tell yourself that you're beautiful even if no one else has the heart to do it. My mom posts notes on my bathroom mirror that remind me that I am beautiful and amazing even when I'm not having a good day. The notes help me to stay motivated and understand that I'm beautiful inside and out no matter what.

Chapter 8
The Rumor of Life

- -

Don't spread with your MOUTH,
What your EYES 👀 didn't see

A rumor is a great way to start an argument and the easiest way to start drama. School wouldn't be school without drama. I go to a school with a decent amount of it. Normally there's someone gossiping, fighting, arguing, or talking about someone else. As much as it's disliked, there's nothing you can do about it.

I heard she was poor

I saw him driving a cab

He goes to the food bank

She is so weird. She watches Star Wars.

Her mom works here thats why she is so "smart"

He doesn't belong here, weirdo

Lying is another really big problem associated with rumors. Lying doesn't help make anyone's life better. If anything, it makes matters worse. I've struggled with trying to tell the truth for a long time. The question is how you program your brain not to have the urge to lie and just want to tell the truth from the start.

I've decided to try a new strategy of telling the truth. The first step is to analyze the situation. In order to prevent lying just think, guess, and breathe: First, I *think* about what I actually did wrong. Then I *guess* what would happen if I lied versus what would happen if I didn't. Lastly, I *breathe* as I realize that telling the truth is the best solution.

Describe a time that you lied to a family member or friend and felt guilty after.

_____

_____

_____

_____

_____

_____

_____

_____

_____

_____

_____

_____

_____

_____

_____

_____

_____

_____

_____

_____

_____

_____

_____

I hate knowing I lied and that I could have avoided a situation overall. Especially when there are consequences to my actions, like phone punishment. Even though you'll still probably be in trouble, you won't have to deal with the guilt of lying.

You should still always do your best, even if you're not the best at something. You'll probably never be *the* best at everything, but you can be *your* best. Always stay true to yourself, and ignore the rumors of life.

Chapter 9

The Gift of Today

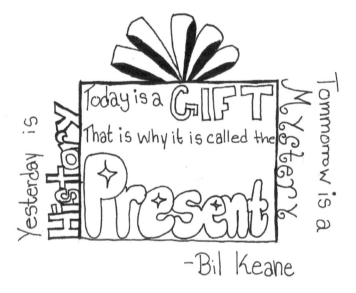

Today is a GIFT
That is why it is called the
Present

Yesterday is History

Tommorrow is a Mystery

—Bil Keane

Everyone is always saying, I can't wait for tomorrow, or yesterday was the best—but what about today? People are so caught up in the future and the past that they can't cherish the present. Remember: "Yesterday's the past, tomorrow's the future, but today is a gift. That's why it's called the present"—Bil Keane, author of the comic strip "The Family Circus."

Understand that today is special and yesterday is gone. Today is here, and we must honor that. People constantly worry about the future but, in reality, all we can do is live in the present, learn from the past, and get ready for the future. God made the world in six days, and everyday he didn't think about what he was going to do the next day; instead, he focused on what he was doing in the moment to successfully complete the world. You must always look at the bright side. My mom always says that every morning, I should look in the mirror and say "something wonderful is going to happen to me"

Name three wonderful things that happened to you today.

1) _____

2) _____

3) _____

I can say from my life experiences that it isn't easy learning and growing as a teen but aim to be yourself, be unique, stay strong and rise above the pink clouds.

About the Author

BréAnna Smith is a fifteen-year-old eleventh grader at Coretta Scott King Young Women's Leadership Academy in Atlanta, Georgia. She's younger than the average eleventh grader because she skipped kindergarden. She's been dancing since age three. She plans to attend Xavier University and become an OB/GYN and work at Grady Hospital. An alternate aspiration is to become the first female African American president of the United States. She loves dancing, running track, reading, writing, shopping, and God. She hopes this book inspires you to rise above the pink clouds.